What is your Prayer?

MARY RUMBLE

Brilliant Books Literary
137 Forest Park Lane Thomasville
North Carolina 27360 USA

What is Your Prayer

What is your prayer?
Is it to be happy and to be of good cheer?
Is it to be successful in life?
Is it to achieve your goals?
Is it to stay in God's will or to stand still?
Is your prayer to be debt free?
What is your prayer?

Don't take no falls, God is always on call
To help you reach your goal,
Stand strong and do not walk away.
God will give you strength to face yet another day.

What is your prayer?
Is it to pray for everyone with love and respect for one another?
Is your prayer to strengthen your faith?
Is your prayer for good health and prosperity?
What is your prayer?
(John 3:1-2)

A Needle in a Haystack

It can be easier to find a needle in a haystack
Than for some Christians to stop being so stubborn.

We, as people, sometimes get into our own selfish ways.
If you take a very strong magnet and turn the haystack
upside down,
Chances are you will get your needle.

If you talk with a very stubborn person and show the love
of God,
With a lot of prayer,
Chances are they might understand.

With that needle, gravity helps pull it down.
Along with time and lots of prayer,
Chances are that stubborn person's mind will change
And blessings will come down.

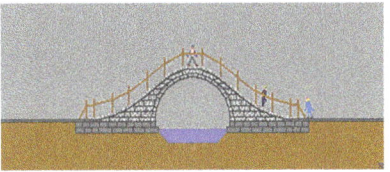

Bridge to Cross

Crossing over your bridge, which has water underneath,
What could be the source of your success?

Crossing over a bridge or a ditch, the process
of leading you to a higher level,
Crossing over that bridge that is above the grass,
We might need to leave some things in the past.

As we live life, we will have some challenges that we are faced with;
Sometimes the biggest bridge is to come face to face with your fears.
We've got to have faith in knowing that God is above all.

Churches

The Bible says "Love your enemy, Love everyone,"
We are not to question God, but question ourselves.
If you make it into heaven, so can your enemy.
Your enemy is not the church or a different religion,
Because we are all sisters and brothers.
We need to learn love from each other.
No one is higher or better than another,
God blessed us with diversity and ambitions
To encourage each other.
Churches, we need to find a common ground;
The enemy is not the TV or radio minister,
They are reaching people that are homebound.
The enemy of the church is the devil;
If he can get God's people fighting against one another,
Then he is happy.
Now the whole world is in trouble.

Conversations

Some people talk about you rather than talk to you;
I realize not everyone is easy to converse with,
Some people talk at you when they are really trying to talk with you.

Everyone is not on the same level, not everyone has the same ethics,
Or have been through the same things in life.

And if you find that it is difficult to communicate to someone,
Then you might want to change your flavor.

Some people might have to be fed with a long-handled spoon;
If people do not like what they are being feed,
They might want to change their diet.

When talking to someone, are you giving
them time to voice their opinions?
To talk at someone could be a form of attacking the person.
We all need to learn better communication skills.
(Proverbs 15:1)

Do You See the Light in the Rain?

When your friends laugh and bring you down,
Leaving you humiliated and in pain,
Can you see the light in the rain?

When your family use and abuse you,
And say that you should be ashamed,
Can you see the light in the rain?

When it seems that all you have done in life
Has pushed you to the ground,
Can you see the light in the rain?

Battle after battle and round after round,
Then look up and realize that
God is that light in the rain.

Don't Choke Me

Don't choke me to be who you want me to be;
If you love me, love me for me.

Don't choke me because you don't understand what I see;
The beauty is everyone has their own unique way.
If you love me, love me for me.

Don't choke me thinking you can take control,
Or tell me what or who I should be.
If you love me, love me for me.

Don't choke me, get to know me for me;
Respect me for me.
If you love me, love me for me.

Everything Was Created from Love

God made the world, he made it all with love,
From Heaven to Earth and everything above,
It all started with God's love.

For God loved us so much that he blessed us with his son,
Who died on the cross.
Jesus paid the price for all.

Jesus rose up so that we all may live.
It is all God's planning, to love all of his creations.
For everything, he gave his love.

(John 3:16)

Face to Face

All of my sins have haunted me;
All of my fears I have faced;
Knowing that God, without a doubt,
 He will work it all out.

All of my enemies have shown their hands and taunted me
With evil they wanted to use against me.
God blessed me to turn it into something positive.

All of the back biting, jealousy, and envy
That are their foolish pride,
I had to face, but they never realized
That God is by my side.

(Isaiah: 54:17)

Fantasy

Like dust that blows along the roads
That is lost and never replaced;
In the midst of time,
A fantasy that I had lost one day,
And yet I stand with memories.

To a fantasy that I had already began to replace once again,
This time with more of a reliable guideline;
Not all fantasy will become real.
For some it is only to give hope
And to others something to live for,
Fantasy helps make some people strong.

Fantasy, without an easy sense of direction,
Just only keep having them;
Fantasy, dreams, thoughts,
For some it just continues to go on,
For others it is a way of turning your dreams into reality.

Fire Flame

A fire flame burns up,
A flame that is burning in your soul,
Because God has taken control.

Praises go up and by keeping the faith,
Blessings come down.
When God has you in his hand,
Everything you do will stand,
What God does for you, no man can touch.

No matter how you turn the fire,
The flame will always burn up.
No matter where you praise God, keeping the faith,
The blessings will come down.

Have You Heard the Wild Birds Sing?

Have you seen the wild birds fight?
God's words said, "If my people, which are called by my name,
Shall humble themselves, and pray and seek my face,
And turn from their wicked ways,
Then will I hear from heaven and will forgive their sin and will heal their land."
(2 Chronicles 7:14)

We, the churches need to come together
And pray for this world.

Then you will hear the wild birds sing
Throughout the whole world.

Hear Why I Cry

O, my God, please hear why I cry.
I know that you do not force your will on us,
But you know what is in our heart.

I cry for the homeless that might be living in the street,
I cry for the motherless and fatherless children,
I cry for the people that do not have any food to eat,
I cry for that person who has lost their job.

I cry for the drug abuser,
I cry for the violence in the schools,
I cry for the sick and the abused.

Heart to Heart

If your heart could look into a mirror, what would it see?
Would it find that it could not understand itself?
Would it find the love that you show to others,
And not that of your sisters or your brothers?

Would it see hatefulness, enviousness, jealousness, and
backbiting?
Would it show the time that you hurt, and the times that
you hurt others?
Would it show that no one cares for the pain that you
once felt?

What would your heart see?
Would it be pleased or would it be full of fears and tears?
Would your heart show the joy, happiness, love,
And encouragement that you have shown to others?
Above all, would it show that you know God?
And that you know how to love others?

Hold to Your Faith

When you feel like your life is in a ship
And a bad storm comes with high waves that you cannot see,
Hold to your faith.

When you feel like everything keeps piling up on you
And your whole world is turning upside down,
Stand on your faith.

When you feel that you are rolling down a hill
And you hit the ground,
Rest in your faith.

In this world today
We need to hold strong to our faith.

How High God Stands

How high up in society can a rich man get?
He spends his money on things he desires
And gets more money anytime he wants.

Even a bird can fly but so high
Before God sends it back down,
And again it has to eat from the ground.

The stars stand high
And the spotlight is on them;
They sometimes give people
Joy, delight, and happiness.

For the stars, they sometime fall, too,
And you can't see their light.

Only God knows how high
A man or things can stand;
And when they fall,
They always ask God, "Why, what was the cause?"

How You Feel

Some people might think that a person is incompetent,
They say the elevator is still stuck in the basement and
don't go up;
When in reality you should be able to see every one as a
human being.

They say that you are not the brightest star in the sky,
They say that you are not normal.
 No one is really normal, it is what is normal for you.

So if people have this perception of you,
That you're someone that other people pass by,
Let them have it because this is who God uses the most.
God can use anyone or even anything,
Sometimes, God will use something or someone small to
confront the wise.

I Am Big and You Are Small

I am big, I am strong,
I can do no wrong.
You are small, you have not a friend, not at all.
Only God is perfect and holds all, the big and the small.

God sees your heart and knows your thoughts.
We might not be judged for our thoughts,
But we will be judged for what's in our hearts.

God knows it's not all about **"I",**
Or how big or small a person appears to be to another.
It is about showing love and caring for each other.
No matter the color, we are all God's children.

I Am Not Ashamed

I am not ashamed anymore that I am hurting,
That reality tries to break my spirit, my faith, my self-esteem.
I am not ashamed because my God stands strong,
He is more than the whole world against me.

They talked about me, laughed at me,
Tried to make me fall.
They thought that they had broken my spirit,
They did not realize that
I was not trying to live my life by man's standards.

I am trying to stay in God's plans.
I am not ashamed because
God removed all of my pain
With his unconditional love.

(Roman's 1:16)

I Don't Care

I don't care what people say.
Sometimes, you have to travel this life by faith.
I don't care what it looks like, sounds like, tastes like or smells like.

I don't care what people think,
You need to learn how to love and trust in God,
Because sometimes He might be the only one you have.

Family sometimes do not understand.
Sometimes you can find more understanding
In a stranger than in a friend.

I don't care what people say,
I don't care what people think,
Time is near for God's return.
Learn how to love and trust in God.

Inner Self

The inner self, the kind that you cannot see,
The words you say that let you know that the inner self
is there.
Sometimes in the inner self, you do things you would not
normally say or do.

With a fast reaction, the inner self sometimes takes control,
And could be sweet or if pushed, very bold.
Like that of two magnetic attractions, in which you will
get some type of reaction,
Like that of humans, if someone attracts you,
You get some kind of reaction.
The inner self, you sometimes might know when it
shows,
The inner self can be the Holy Ghost.

It's All Out in the Open

It's all out in the open now.
If the devil knew who Jesus was before He died on the cross
Then Jesus might not have been crucified.

If man understood one another,
Then they would stop being abusive,
Lying, and cheating, and being so confused.

Do not let your left hand know what your right hand is doing.
If you let everyone know what you are doing, you might not achieve your dreams.
People might not kill you, but they will kill your dreams with the words they say.

It's all out in the open.
The devil comes to steal, kill and destroy.
In the end, God wins.
If you are living by God's word, your battle has already been won.

Matthew 6:3

Joy Street

Joy Street is living where your life is a success,
By being happy and being alive.
On this street there can be a few bumps and bruises,
But you still keep the joy.

Joy is when you have the wisdom and the strength
To go through life knowing that you can face the game.
On this street there might be hills, mountains, and curves.
You keep moving, never giving in to the pain.
Joy Street is keeping your faith and trusting in God.

Keeping Your Faith

When you are in God's will, God has his hands on you.
The devil might try to do something to discourage you.
Keep living by God's words, because God will make the
devil pay.

Things might look bad, but what people don't understand
Is that something negative can be turned into something
positive.

If you have been fighting from day to day,
Knowing that you have reached the point

That you don't care what people say,
Keep the faith, knowing that God has a Blessing on the way.
Stand strong, you will not go wrong in keeping your
faith.

Let the Leaves Fall

Let the leaves fall;

As a leaf falls on the ground,

It waits patiently for God to come and move it away, mostly with the wind.

A car or person might come and move those leaves away.

Just as a person can fail as they try to reach their goals,

Sometimes God will send a stranger to help them to achieve their dreams.

Let the leaves fall.

Leaves can sometimes get mushy or crumbled up on the ground.

Leaves have seasons, just as people have seasons,

When they rise or fall.

Only God knows the time, reason, and call.

Let Us Praise God

We all do not praise God the same;
Some praise with dance, some with a song.
The culture of some and the ethics of others,
We all are not the same.

Some praise with tears, some with laughter;
The pride of some and the joy of others.
Some praise with clapping, some with hands lifted up,
The wisdom of some and the respect of others.

Some praise with music, some with shouting.
We all need to understand that in God's sight
We all are sisters and brothers.
No matter the creed and no matter the color.

"Let everything that has breath praise the Lord."

(Psalm 150:6)

Life Observer

Can a man judge a book before he reads it?
Can a man judge a person that he just met?
Life Observer, you too, even have someone judging you.

It may not be by man's standard, but by God's planning,
To judge others without a cause,
Knowing that God has individually blessed us all with
different characteristics.

As humans, the fear is trying to judge
What we don't understand.
May God bless us to learn from each other,
No matter the color.
You cannot measure nor judge what God does for others.

You have to trust and know that God will bless you, too.
God is in control.

Love and Jealousy

Love for your parents,
Love for your sisters and brothers,
But unfortunately, sometimes sisters and brothers can be
jealous of one another.

To be loved is sometimes great;
It can cause a lost person to find themselves once again
And a half-dying person to want to live again.

Love is often cherished for a few years.
If it is not strong, then it turns old,
And will cause one to walk out the door;
That can sometimes hurt more than just those two people.

With no communication and the lack of understanding,
The appearance of another and the jealousy of the other,
Hiding jealousy over and over again,
Forces the love to end.

You can love someone and yet never have to commit a sin,
And only be their close friend.
Love like that is what the whole world needs more of.

To love and cherish one another,
Even if there are disagreements at times,
Love like that is stronger than gold,
For it comes from one's soul
And has no end.

Having jealousy can bring humiliation and pain;
All love is not the same,
So think twice before you call it a game
Because love can bring a million things.

Man to Man

Man can be the smartest creature with high technology and schooling.
Man, oh man, man can also be the saddest creature.

Due to life's battles, flaws and feeling that
life is too much of a challenge,
Man to man, man can be the loneliest creature.

No friends, no plans, no understanding,
Not understanding that man can live in God's plan.
Every man is formed in God's image.

(Genesis 1:26)

My Child

You were born with a precious gift from God.
I know that life can be a little struggle,
My child, God is by your side always.
                    Persevere!

My child, focus on what you want in life.
God will bless you, have patience, faith and trust
Knowing that God will bless you through it all.

Never give up your dreams,
Do not let anyone try to take them away from you.
                    Persevere!

My Prayer

Oh, my Lord, my mind is heavy,
And my heart is bare,
Time and space go around and around.

Oh, my God, people do not have any love for one another,
Not even their own sister or brother.

If history is repeating itself,
Then the whole world is in trouble,
People killing each other.

Oh, my God, I think if we humble ourselves,
And use the strength of prayer,
We can change this world.

(2 Chronicles 7:14)

Oh, My God

I thank you, God.
When I was in bondage,
You brought me out.
When I was in prison you gave me strength.
When I was in chains you blessed me with time.
When I was in pain, you healed me.
With each step I have taken, you were there.
Thank you, God.

(Psalm: 139)

Persecuted to God's Miraculous Movement

Jesus, my God, I feel like I'm being persecuted.
Beasts I have faced, beasts my God has killed.
God will not put any more on you than you can bear.

When I was surrounded by a stone mountain on every side,
I thought that I would fold.
God came and showed me that sometimes you have to
be bold.

The burdens of my past let me know that
God is stronger than the whole world against me.
Persecuted to God's miraculous movement.

Privilege

As humans we all do not have the same understanding,
But we all have the same privilege.
The privilege of living.

Life seems to be a battle for some
And a trap or game for others,
Even a big gamble for some
But yet for all, it is a privilege.

For some with a key to where it begins
But without an understanding or reason to why it ends,
Because God never fails, but man fail God.

The privilege of being loved,
The privilege of happiness, sharing your love with others
The privilege of living from day to day.

The world has a lot of manipulative tools,
That can leave some very confused,
We have the privilege to turn to God
And let God guide us.

The privilege of being alive,
Privilege of knowing that God will provide,
The privilege of having different characteristics
The privilege of knowing that God holds all of life in existence.

We all have the privilege to have God by our side,
But because we are humans, we all do not understand.

Searching Heart

Born a child, in search of a meaning to my existence;
Whose child am I?

Searching through yesterday's pains,
Today's dreams and tomorrow's thoughts,
For happiness I once knew as a child.

Not knowing feelings of fear, color or strength,
Not knowing judgment or wealth,
But knowing that God above gives all of us his precious love.

Yes, Lord, I have a searching heart,
For the happiness that lives deep within,
Because that is the reason to life in existence.

The happiness that everyone has,
The reason why each person is,
That precious gift from heaven above
Which is God's unconditional love.

Storms

Sometimes you need to walk in your storms.
Some storms you need to pray about,
Some storms you need to be still in,
Some storms you need to move away from,
Some storms you need to forgive.

Behind most storms there is a change, especially if there
were strong winds or rain.
Behind rain, things often grow;
With strong winds things might fall down or change.

Only God knows what a storm will bring and how it
might affect you.
Trust in God and God will bring you through it.

Survive

Survival is not a game,
It can be so much pain.
To bully someone is very cruel,
You might think that you are getting away.

God is the timekeeper,
Only God knows when you will reap what you have
sown.
Survive your struggles and your falls,
Know that through it all, God will strengthen you.

Survive when everyone around you
Thinks what you've been through is funny.
They don't know how God will bless you.

Tears

For every teardrop that falls from your eyes,
God knows the reason and why.

Be patient and humble yourself,
Stay in God's will, because he has your reward.

For every teardrop of pain,
God will bless you with strength.

For every teardrop of sorrow,
God will continue to comfort you.

For every teardrop of fear,
God will bless you with courage.

For every teardrop of joy,
God has shown that he is with you through it all.

The Forest Runs Deep

When the trees praise God,
It does not matter if it is a pine tree next to a cedar tree;
They all sing and praise God together.

The forest runs deep,
Together the trees stand strong and tall,
Together they face the storms.

Each branch is different from the other branch
And yet they praise God with a new song,
From the trunk to the full height of the tree,
Together they stand to protect what is growing beneath.

The Village

When I was little, young, and confused,
And did not understand,
The village showed me love and courage.

As a young lady, so full of energy and strength,
The village showed me wisdom and kindness.

And as I moved away from my village,
I learned that life can be cruel and so unkind;
Then I would stop and think to myself,

Thank God for the village
And the lessons they taught me,
That of character and integrity.

The Wind Blows

Wind, you cannot see it but you can feel it;
Yet it can be so strong that it can blow things away or knock things over.
Faith, the size of a grain of a mustard seed,
Faith is something you can feel in your heart and know you have it.

Having faith that is strong as the wind,
Can move mountains and build things,
And give you the courage to achieve your dreams.

A nice calm wind, and a nice cool breeze,
like that of immeasurable faith;
Wind can sometimes be cold, having strong faith
means that you sometimes have to be bold.

Wind is blind, faith is blind; you just have to keep giving God the glory.

(Luke 17:6)

Walk in the Dark

How far can you walk in the dark and not in a park?
How far can you walk in blindness; or walk in trust, faith and understanding?
Do you give love and show respect for others?

How far can you walk in confusion, abusiveness, and fear?
How far can you walk in the rain, not showing your pain?
How far can you walk having fears and tears and life's worries and stresses?

Would you walk straight, or would you wobble to the left or to the right
Or keep up your good fight?
Would you walk with grace, honor, and courage knowing that God is ordering your steps?
How far can you walk in the dark?
Know that Jesus is the Light of the World, and He can lead the way.

John 8: 12

Who Laughs the Longest?

You laughed at me, said I was a fool.
Things in life don't just happen in small cities but all
around the world.
You said that I am poor and you don't know where I
came from.
We do not all have the same ethics or goals.

When you laugh and criticize others,
You are only hurting yourself.
You keep laughing and God will keep blessing me;
I am not saying that you cannot laugh,
Because sometimes people need a good laugh in life;

Just be careful how you laugh at others.
You do not know the plans God has for someone's life,
Or who God will use and how he will use them.
We are all God's vessels and his tools.
Sometimes tools get beaten down.
God comes in, polishes them up, and lets them shine.

Who's Your Friend?

Who is your friend?
Someone that prays for you or someone that prays about you?

Some friends you can keep close and some you cannot keep close;
Some will be paper thin, some cannot hold water, and some will bend.

Everyone you call a friend is not your friend.
Some people want things from you,
Only a few want things for you.

A true friend can tell you things that might hurt you;
But it is something that will help you to be strong.

Walk a Mile

I cannot walk a mile in your shoes and you cannot walk
a mile in mine.
Sometimes you have to crawl before you can walk.
Sometimes people need to think before they talk.

We, as people, may go through some hardships in life;
That is when we need to help a friend out by showing
love, support and understanding.

As you take that mile walk, walk with faith and courage,
Let God lead the way.
(Proverbs: 3 and 5)

Your Lawn

Cutting your grass and looking at your life;
People love for their lawn to look good and nice.
What about your life?

You can take short cuts to cutting your grass,
Just as you can take short cuts in your life and make it shorter;
High, wild growing grass; like that of a person's life, out of control.

Grass can have different shapes and different colors, just like people;
However, with grass, we realize that it is all equal.

Most people make a path or trail when cutting
grass; Just as there is a path to life;
Live your life with God's master plan, by
staying in God's will for your life.

Anger and Danger

Anger, the longer you hold it, the more it grows;
Playing with your intelligence, trying to take control.
In anger there is a lot of pain, feeling empty, lost, or confused,
Sometimes even feeling abused.

Consistently lying, comparing, competing, and instigating;
Anger has no respect of color.
Anger can become dangerous and unhealthy for you, not
knowing how to release it.

Anger and danger running out of control,
With prayer, repentance, and learning to forgive,
Put everything in God's hand and he will take control.

A Silent Praise

When you are covered with God's grace and walking in faith,
Give God your silent praise.
Not everyone can talk or walk,
God knows what is in your heart.

That silent praise will be heard by God;
Man cannot always understand someone else's heart.

God knows the challenges that you have to face,
God will bring you through life's challenges.
Just keep praising God.
Just keep praising God.

As the World Turns

As the world turns,
Things are not always like what they appear to be;
People in pain, babies and children crying
No one cares to take the blame.
The world is moving fast,
Is anyone taking the time for prayer?

As the world turns,
Are we living as God created us to live?
Have we forgotten God's Master Plan?
Are we a world that just does not care about hardship and pain?

As the world turns,
God blesses us to see yet another day.
The world needs to be thankful for God's Grace.

God's Will

The time is here, judge yourself;
God's will for each and every one is more than my words
can say.
Where violence is, love needs to speak.

People are afraid of how other people feel about them.
People can only have the power that you allow them to
have over you.
It is God's will we should seek, to overcome the violence
of the day.

Be bold, be strong, God is in control.
We need to seek God's will for our lives
And know that God will provide.

Autobiography of Mary Rumble Flemming

I was born in Northeastern North Carolina. I am the youngest of six children born to the late Elmer Lee (Bus) Rumble and Melinda Felton Rumble. I was born in Chowan County, but later on my parents moved to Perquimans County. I spent my childhood basically in what I call Perq/Chow County. As a child, I enjoyed playing with my siblings and working in the garden with my father and siblings. Going to church with my parents was a big part of my life. Different family members would tell us their favorite Bible story.

My love for poetry developed when I was in sixth grade. My teacher would give us poems by various authors on Monday and we would have to recite the poems each Friday. It was then that I developed my appreciation of poetry. Years later, after I graduated from high school, I started writing poems on my own. Sometimes, I would recite my poems to different family members.

After graduating from high school, I lived in several places. After getting married, I moved to Milwaukee, Wisconsin where I live for twenty one years. I am the mother of two biological adult sons and two other sons.

In 2014, God blessed me to return to North Carolina to take care of my mother. Once back home in Northeastern North Carolina, I was able to recapture my first love, writing poetry.

I thank God, my parents, and my "Village" for what they instilled in me as I was growing up and for any success that I have achieved in my life today.

www.ingramcontent.com/pod-product-compliance
Lightning Source LLC
Chambersburg PA
CBHW051246120626
46547CB00014B/1812